The Tenets of Dmitrism

By: Dmitri Brooksfield

LIBERTY UNDER ATTACK PUBLICATIONS

Publisher Information:
Website: www.libertyunderattack.com
Contact: shane@libertyunderattack.com

Cover Design By: Miriam Zachariah
Interior Design By: Shane Radliff

Published By *Liberty Under Attack Publications*, March 2023

Table of Contents

First Tenet: Ideological Purity

"Mentis puritas super omnia"

The first of Dmitrism's main tenants is one of purity. That being of Ideology. The Dmitrist remains pure in ideological conviction, and resists being swayed by the inferior pseudo-caste of ideologies which have proven themselves the enemy of the Dmitrist.

Statism (be it fascism, communism, or modern liberalism) being the chief example of impurities which must be debated and refuted at all chances wherever it crops up. This is just a taste of the many enemies of the Dmitrist and his fellow libertarian allies.

The Dmitrist must prove himself a one-man vanguard against ideological heresies at all times and be willing to debate them peacefully to starve them of nearby converts when possible, and destroy them if they dare to come in the form of the initiation of force towards the peaceful and pacifist. The Dmitrist destroys these violent foes with a righteous fire in his heart and a bayonet on his rifle, as the Dmitrist must dislike the statist by nature, and must wish to destroy the statist who brings death and violence to his and his neighbors door. To bring aggression against the peaceful and innocent is dishonorable, and proof of one's impure ideology or ideological consistency. The statist is not evil by nature, only when he turns to force and aggression does he become the evil the Dmitrist must destroy.

The Dmitrist prefers non-violent means to erase inferior ideologies, and thus must hone his debate and refutation skills, educate himself with all he can, on both his own arguments and the arguments his opponent will bring forth in all likelihood. The Dmitrist must not fear reading the works and theories of other ideologies, he must know all he can to bring those of inferior ideologies into the fold, born anew into libertarianism. To tolerate these inferiors and not be tormented or swayed by them is proof of the ideological consistency, purity, and superiority of libertarianism and Dmitrism itself. It bears repeating,the only time inferior systems of thought are intolerable is when aggression is involved; if a man of another ideology commits a criminal act, he is not to be tolerated and must be dealt with swiftly and justly in accordance with the libertarian principle of proportionality to obtain a proper counterfactual and to right past wrongs.

The Dmitrist also understands that other libertarian creeds are similar to his but with varying degrees of degeneracy, such as the Georgists and the Objectivists, who both believe in minarchism. But the Dmitrist knows still that they are at least libertarian in nature, and will follow the NAP to its logical conclusion if not by themselves, then by experience.

Second Tenet: Labor

"Qui multum laborat, bene manducat"

The Dmitrist knows that hard work makes a man healthy, makes a man happy, and makes a man proud of his accomplishments. While idly passing time in leisure is fine as well, working in the fields or factories are not only industrious and productive, they also provide for the Dmitrist a sense of self that is hard to obtain. The Dmitrist senses that he is part of a machine of industry, making products and food for the society he lives in, helping to ensure that the hungry are fed and the clothless become clothed.

He is a proud man, a working man, a member of the libertarian proletariat, taking up a small but important role in his society, for not only his own gain with payment but the gain of those who want the works he helped produce. In this, the Dmitrist enshrines himself as a pillar of the workforce, and stands strong alongside his peers in industrious unity. The statists do not understand the meaning of hard work, for they prefer to shrug off such things, instead choosing a desk or a camera over the hands-on and laborious tasks that the Dmitrist willingly and joyfully takes into his own hands. They cannot understand the united struggle all Dmitrists and libertarians partake in to better not just themselves but also the society as a whole.

The libertarian proletariat is not the only kind of worker however, for there are many facets to a society. The entrepreneurs, those in teamster occupations, retail and fast food, the savvy investor, and the construction worker are all united hand-in-hand to make the society prosper and grow: never mock them, never insult your fellow libertarian for the job he keeps, for he is contributing just as you are. Instead, be grateful for his productivity, his willingness to keep the engines of industry running in his own way.

And if the statist wishes to join this front, to help contribute after years of slothfulness, let him, so he may prove himself worthy of being considered part of the libertarian proletariat front and learn as the Dmitrist has learned. Namely, that hard work is happy work, that hard work is proud work, And most of all, Hard work is honest work.

The Dmitrist must learn to plant foods, to grow them, to harvest them, and to sell them. He must learn the ways of the 'green-thumb' and be self-sufficient in times of hardship and hunger, to be able to survive and thrive when the going gets tough. He must know these things to feed himself and his family, his neighbors and peers. To make a surplus where there is a shortage and to invest his profits methodically and intelligently wherever possible.

Third Tenet: Militarism

"Ense petit placidam sub libertate quietem"

The Dmitrist must foster a society ready to both defend itself and its people, as well as prepare for the liberation of the oppressed Dmitrists and libertarians around the world. The Dmitrist knows that his comrades are counting on him to bear the rifle and the saber alongside them in the trenches or on the beaches. Dmitrism cannot be protected solely by words alone, it must be guarded by a mighty pen, yes, but also a shield and a sword and a spear.

The good Dmitrist teaches his peers to defend themselves if they are uneducated, and teaches them to fight from the bushes as a guerrilla rather than a statist soldier who uses inferior 'conventional' tactics reserved for the imperialists armies. The Dmitrist learns from a young age to fire a rifle, a pistol, and a mortar, and takes these teachings to heart.

He learns bushcraft, fortification, weapon assembly and disassembly, cleaning and maintenance, and to hunt and forage for food as to survive in the harshness of the war theater. A good Dmitrist uses his knowledge and passes these skills down to his posterity when he can and at a steady pace. With these skills, he will become a member of a society of warriors and militants ready at a minute's notice to defend said society. The Dmitrists of a libertarian society should set up volunteer corps. So that every man who wishes to liberate the libertarian globally may do so on his own volition.

They should coordinate to spread propaganda around the world in times of peace and use force in times of liberation to defend the innocent and the victimized. A 'time of liberation' is when the Dmitrist is joined by other libertarians to put an end to evil deeds wherever and whenever they arise. Be it genocide, mass purges, or mass incarceration of the innocent. The Dmitrists will fight to defend those who are victims of oppression, and liberate said victims so they may govern themselves. The Dmitrists will also do all they can to spread the good word of Dmitrism in every land they liberate through propaganda, debate, and fiery orations.

It is important to always remember the golden rule of libertarianism in times of necessary violence,:the Dmitrist never harms the innocent himself, and will do all he can to protect them if they are in harm's way. This way, the Dmitrist is a savior, a beacon of liberty in a world gone mad and bleak. He will always and forever do good unto others for the same in return. He will provide aid to those who are injured and alms to the hungry, sick, and the cold. The Dmitrist in essence is "The Libertarian Man" and a representative of libertarianism everywhere it spreads.

The man of the future, Today.

Fourth Tenet: Industrial-Agrarianism

"planta una manu, altera aedifica"

The society of Dmitrism must be one of two parts. One part is agricultural and the other is industrial, and both are necessary for society to prosper. The inferior ideologies of the past have chosen one over the other to bring prosperity to their lands, but have found only death and want instead. The Dmitrist society should have private farms and ranches in the fertile lands within the boundaries the society claims, and in the non-fertile areas, there should be private factories, mills, and all manner of production. The oceansides, if any are present, should be home to fisheries and hatcheries so as to further increase food production. It should also be noted that this can only be done in the libertarian manner, that being in accordance to the principle of private property, and no coercion may be permitted to do this; the Dmitrist is above command-economics and the inferior creeds of the statist vampire economies of the past.

The good Dmitrist understands that in all things, perfection is impossible, this includes a laissez-faire market economy, but he makes do with what is available to him and his comrades and within the parameters allowed by the principles that guide him. A factory or two within a fertile valley, or a farm on the roof of an inner-city house is but a trivial matter that is not important in the long run. The Dmitrist is more concerned with having adequate amounts of both locally consumed food and cash profit exports of goods, as these aid in the growth of society and are far more attention focused.

The good Dmitrist factory worker works hard to make shoes for local consumption and for export so he may be paid for his labor, the Dmitrist farmer works hard to grow food for his family and to sell to his village or to a factory for canning for further export. The CEO works hard to increase his companies profits and the efficiency of his workers, while the rancher works hard to care for and protect his herd so as to produce meat and milk and cheeses.

The free market is how the libertarian thrives, and the Dmitrist knows and adopts this, as he knows it to be self-evident upon seeing it in action. The invisible hand of the market operates continuously and without a guiding central plan, and over time society benefits from such anarchy of industry and agriculture. The Dmitrist protects this always through his hard labor and good output, and never through intervention in the market through force or coercion. For as said before, that is the way of the statist, and the statist has shown himself to be folly in many ways, this being one of them. The only 'fair' is laissez-faire, always and forever.

Fifth Tenet: The New Propaganda

"bellum verbis, bellum animis"

The inferior philosophies that surround us are always trying to win over converts through lies, deception, and trickery. The Dmitrist is not swayed by these foolish attempts at opinion molding, instead he harnesses his might and principled worldview to stave off these hideous lies. He uses this power to create a new form of propaganda, one which uses bits and pieces of the old and inferior forms, and melding it to a new way of enticing people to join Dmitrism and libertarianism.

This 'new propaganda' uses facts, logic, and observable conditions to sway opinion in the direction of the Dmitrist while also using pleasant and eye-drawing aesthetics. The Dmitrists propaganda should be principled, using slogans and data that support its causes and ideals, it should be clear and easy to understand. Posters, billboards, songs, slogans, and flags; all are viable options for the Dmitrist to spread his message. The use of pamphlets and flyers are always acceptable for this task. The giving of this very manifesto from which you read now to another, or the passing out of copies, furthers the goals of Dmitrism, as what better way to spread it than letting others read the tenants for themselves?

The aesthetics of Dmitrism should be used in this propaganda to help viewers easily identify Dmitrism as the movement grows. The Symbol of Dmitrism (the eye of vigilance within the sun sporting an iris in the shape of an anarchist 'A') is a proud symbol, and can easily stand out in the most obscure of places wherever it may be found. The Dmitrist wears the symbol with honor as if it were a badge representing the way forward, a future for all mankind and all libertarians.

The Propaganda of the Dmitrist should be placed wherever possible within reason, he must make sure to never violate the property rights of others to do this for that is unprincipled. Always respect the property rights of other men, even if those men are of inferior ideology,. After all, you are trying to bring others into the fold not scare them away with unwarranted hostilities. The Colors of libertarianism and Dmitrism (gold and black) should be used often and used to ingrain within all who see them, the thought of libertarianism and Dmitrism. Dmitrists are individuals, so choosing a style of art for visual propaganda is up to them on their own opinions, but borrowing from older and inferior ideologies such as communism, jingoism and republicanism, would serve the Dmitrist well in the long run. Not only are these styles attention grabbing, they also can be used to convey messages with a powerful visual aid.

Sixth Tenet: Health Of The Dmitrist

"Curre, salire, scande, pugna, cogita"

The Dmitrist prides himself on being able to do labor, and works hard wherever and whenever possible to increase his stamina, strength, and internal health. Dmitrism is an ideology of work and militancy, and as such requires the Dmitrist to work on himself as soon as possible, to become strong and brave and healthy in multiple ways. The Dmitrist may do physical exercise such as running, rock climbing, weights, yoga, sit-ups and push-ups to increase his fitness of the body. He may also eat healthier foods or diet on occasion to help his internal health and digestion, and he may also refuse to do drugs, alcohol, or smoke to prevent harming his innards.

The Dmitrist might read books, write papers and essays, watch documentaries in his free time, and digest the information within them to increase his mental health and knowledge. He may even do meditation to clear this thoughts from time-to-time. All of these and many more are ways the Dmitrist may begin and continue to increase his health and further help the cause by becoming "The Libertarian Man" over time. The Libertarian Man is the peak of the libertarians pride, he has become a strong, capable, and industrious fellow ready to do the hard labor, prepared to defend his family and homeland, and has a wit and intelligence to dismantle any inferior ideology who crosses him in the debate hall.

The Dmitrist knows he cannot obtain perfection in all these things, but nonetheless does all he can to achieve as much as he can, to be the best he can be. There is no higher honor than that which you bestow upon yourself, the words "I succeeded". The Dmitrist does all he can to boost the charisma and morale of his fellow libertarians, pushing them forward with a strong resolve. He willingly aids the weaker Dmitrists and libertarians to become healthier, to bring them up to his level and welcome him not only as a brother, but as a fellow of good health, both in body and mind. In a Dmitrist society, gymnasiums would prove useful ventures for entrepreneurs, as would libraries. For the thirst for gains and knowledge will inevitably be in high demand by the Dmitrist and the libertarian alike.

Seventh Tenet: Dealing With Other Anarchists

"leniter ambulare sed portare magnum lignum"

The Dmitrist knows that he is not the only anarchist and libertarian out there, and he also understands that the other anarchists have varying differences of ideology and some with similar levels of degeneracy as other libertarian creeds. He does not fault them for such misguided ideas, he wishes them the best on their attempts at trying to bring their ideas into reality and moves on or tries to persuade them to give up on such follies through reason, debate, and logic.

The Dmitrist does not feel hard feelings towards other anarchists, but treats them similarly to libertarian creeds he is used to, perceiving them as simply another group to try and reason with. He does not lose hope on them when his attempts at persuasion are met with scorn or contempt by other ideologies as this is a given, they are simply stubborn or filled with propaganda of the bygone ages before them. The old believers will either convert or such ideas will die out with the passing of the elderly of said ideology.

As said before, the Dmitrist knows that some of these anarchists hold degenerate beliefs such as the abolition of private property, and the allowance of planned economies. He is not worried though, as he is a Dmitrist by his own volition and is a mighty bulwark against those parasitic ideas. He is already vigilant and prepared to root out those who try to use any coercion or violence to enforce those ideas on those in the Dmitrist or libertarian society. The Dmitrist is an anarchist, and thus sees all forms of statism as inferior systems of vampire economics, society building, and authority worship. He can easily dismantle all these with relative ease and by using the statists' logic against them.

Dmitrists know that power corrupts anything it touches, and even the most pure of heart cannot control his urges and temptations when provided an outlet for authority via the state apparatus. He sees the state for what it is, not only a parasite, but an inferior form of society organization and control which is outdated, immoral, and illegitimate by all standards. The Dmitrist in this can sympathize with other anarchist factions who also see this truth, and will be able to use this kindred knowledge to help him sway said anarchists to his aid or position.

Eighth Tenet: Virtuanism

"Esto benignus, adiuva infirmos, loquere pauperibus, benefac"

The Earth has many people, some good and evil, some kind hearted and cruel. The Dmitrist knows this to be so and does his greatest wherever possible to alleviate the suffering of others with little or no gain for himself. He is a man of justice in this respect, for he sees the plights of mankind and the failures of the inferior ideologies and wishes to write the wrongs of the past done in the names of these creeds of old. He is a passionate man who is not afraid to shed tears when faced with the sorrows and failed hopes or dreams of those he comes across. He does what he can to aid said people as he is able to. He may feed the hungry, nurse the sick, repair that which is damaged and so forth.

The Dmitrist is a man who has a powerful urge to do good unto others and to move society forward for all humanity. He knows that he cannot save the world all on his own, though he wants to dearly. The Dmitrist unites with the libertarian proletariat to do the hard work of society and to help the less fortunate. This is what is called 'Virtuanism', which means a society of virtuous people, a single Dmitrist who is virtuous is called a 'Virtuan' in this respect.

The good Dmitrist follows the principles of right-libertarianism in his ethics and morality, chiefly amongst these is the 'golden rule' which is described as "treat others as you yourself wish to be treated". The Dmitrist also follows the Non Aggression Principle for the same reason. Although the Statist doesn't follow the same ideology as the Dmitrist, they are also to be given this respect, for they are still human.

The Dmitrist wants to see a world filled with kindness, love and respect and will foster this attitude amongst himself and his peers, for he knows a polite society is a healthy society and a healthy society is one the Dmitrist desires. The Dmitrist doesn't bother with societal issues such as homosexuality or religion, for he shouldn't care what another man does as long as he is bringing harm to nobody but himself or willing adult parties. In this regard he still follows the principles set forth by libertarianism, which can be summed up as "Live and let live". A Dmitrist can be homosexual, heterosexual, or even asexual. He may be Christian, Jew, Muslim, or Atheist. The Dmitrist does not judge on lifestyle, religion or sexual preference alone; he judges other humans on the basis of actions taken and desires in society. A Muslim pacifist is not a problem, while an openly violent Christian may be a problem. The Dmitrist is always vigilant to spot aggressors and deal with them, so as to help keep society safe and calm. In time, all people will melt together in kinship and assimilation, and Muslims, Jews, Christians, and all others of every race, religion, and sexual preference will live in natural harmony as mankind, unified.

Ninth Tenet: The Libertarian Question

"non pugnabis ultra, iunges manus et ad astra peruenias"

The Dmitrist is surrounded by ideologies on all sides in the modern age, from the fascist to the monarchist. He knows that, in all likelihood, they will be around until they die out from lack of support, or by being debated and erased over time by the Dmitrist. The libertarians however are a different story, as many kinds coexist alongside Dmitrism. Although peppered with glaring issues and degeneracies, the Dmitrist is fine with tolerating these libertarian creeds as they mean him no harm and are likely to provide gallant allies and friends from the ranks of said ideologies in the seemingly never ending war against statism.

The libertarian question, as is now dubbed, can be answered quite well by finding out what that question is. That question which the Dmitrist knows is "shall we join hands with them?" and the answer to that is 'yes'. The Dmitrist is pure in conviction, pure in ideology and will be able to ally with such libertarians as the Objectivists, Voluntaryists, Hoppeans and all else in a union of libertarianism which will push us towards 'our dream' and a better society for all humankind. The Dmitrist follows all if not most of the libertarian principles that they all follow, so coming together is something the Dmitrist is open to in times of necessity.

The Dmitrist is a man of principle and purity above all else though, and rejects the idea of 'political pragmatism', and instead stands strong with rigid ideological conviction. He is merely allying with these libertarians, he will not allow their degeneracy to worm its way into his worldview. The Dmitrist must not allow the degradation of his society through the melding of lesser ideologies together. He is aware that slip-ups may occur as all Dmitrists are human, but they must remain as vigilant as possible to always correct these issues wherever they pop up through careful debate and reassurance.

A Dmitrist rejects all forms of governance, all forms of taxation, and all forms of conscription. He must never fall to these temptations as they spell the doom of all civilized societies who adopt them. Dmitrism shall be the purest of libertarian ideologies in the end, so the Dmitrist has only to push forward society in the ways a Dmitrist should and the world will follow if not by example then by debate, propaganda, and refutation.

Tenth Tenet: Our Dream

"Ad astra, omnes homines"

The Dmitrist has a dream, that one day Dmitrism shall cover the earth in glorious liberty and prosperity. He dreams of a world united not by force, fear, or governance. But instead a world united by the Dmitrist creed and by a passion to expand and discover and reach to the stars, to inherit the skies as mankind's birthright. Many people under other ideologies were promised the false hope of living amongst the stars with their families, where the evil of statism, poverty, and hunger couldn't reach them. The Dmitrist feels tears welling up in him whenever he sees the downtrodden and the disheartened who the communists, fascists, and republicans left behind as the space race era ended and died. Those soviet citizens who were promised a dream, whose entire lives were spent in poverty, grueling oppression, and hunger, who grew up being told that 'some day our dream will come, young child' and yet whose dreams were dashed by reality.

The Dmitrist wishes to right this wrong, and this is the ultimate goal of the Dmitrist. The Dream that a united, libertarian, free earth, will lay down their guns, hold hands, and look up to the skies. The Dmitrists will look at the stars and fulfill the ultimate dream of our species. But to do this the Dmitrist must work hard to improve himself, his society, and to unite the earth under the black banner of Dmitrism, he must do his part to bring forth this dream for all his peers, his posterity, and his ancestors' memories. The millions whose tears were shed, blood was spilled, and bodies starved are looking upon you, Dmitrist.

Will you let the dream of a united earth die, like the dreams of so many others? Will you let the stars remain a dim beacon in the night, where no man may travel?

Or will you as a man, nay, a human being; raise your hands to the night sky and yell "Our Dream Lives on!" Do not let the embers of that dream die, Dmitrist. Do your part, stand as a comrade with your fellow Dmitrists, and bring forth a new age of love, tolerance, unity, and prosperity to all of mankind. Imagine yourself, walking upon a foreign planet, or aboard a space station looking down upon our little blue ball, imagine yourself on a space walk, meeting other species, colonizing other worlds. And for all that is righteous, once more raise your hands to the stars, ball them into fists, and shout with conviction, fervor, and truth in your voice.

"Our Dream lives on!"

Our dream lives on....

Embers

A Poem By Dmitri Brooksfield

Embers of a bygone day, blowing away from the
wildfires ruin A tear shed for the devastation within our
hearts, ambition lost A dream that never was, lost to
times far behind
A child with a toy rocket, they drop it to the ground to
stare above The night glows bright, candles in the
dimness, the sea of suns and earths beyond The embers
enter now, and blow upon the toy rocket, its engines
ignite Away it flies to the the abyss of darkness, and the
night sky is lit bright now,
The child dreams asleep, helmet upon her head, she
sees the world that could be
As we should be, as one, a sea of suits, marching
aboard a silver ship to the stars
A line of orange and white flooding the corridors,
No flags, no letters, all as one mankind, one mission to
the heavens
This, she says to herself, is the dream I wanted
Our dream.

Notes From Dmitri Brooksfield

I am Dmitri Brooksfield, the man behind this new ideological crusade against the statist and his ilk. I have decided that I need to address the readers directly as to convey my personal thoughts for all to see. The Tenets of Dmitrism are what I envision the libertarian of the future to be part of, a unified front of liberty-minded purists, a mighty bulwark against the continuing libertine influences that have degraded libertarianism into a bad joke amongst older and inferior ideologies. We live in a cruel and dark age, where men rape, murder, torture, and war with each other over petty differences in race, religion, sexual orientation, and ideology.

I reject this world's finality.

We cannot stand idly by while mankind's dreams and aspirations of peace, harmony, and expansion are allowed to be extinguished like the embers of a dying fire. I made this new creed as a way to right past wrongs of the libertarian front. Seeing the moral and ethical collapse of libertarianism into a mess of squabbling minarchists, libertines, junkies, and socialists has angered me greatly. We used to be the only ones who wanted truth and justice to prevail, for liberty to return to all of us. Now though, power and politics have corrupted our message. I wish for Dmitrism to spread globally, to reignite the flames of liberty, to purify the corruption and to unite mankind under a peaceful world where mankind can focus on its dreams of living amongst the stars.

I also have to write down some information I think is equally important, regarding myself. I, ever since thinking and creating the tenants of Dmitrism, have been trying to enact them in my own life. I exercise more, I eat less, I've switched from sugar in my coffee to alternatives, I've meditated and lost some weight, I've read more books of both libertarian theory and the theory of other ideologies. I wish to become the Libertarian Man to the best of my ability, and I aspire to become a pillar of this new world that the Dmitrist wants to uphold. Every now and then I falter, I fail at my goals; but this is nothing to be ashamed of, instead you must learn from mistakes and try again, and when more people accept Dmitrism, there will be many who will help you back on your feet. The Dmitrist is a kind soul who wants to help his peers to become the best he can be through encouragement and boosting of morale.

This is the way to success my friends, I tell you this. There is no better feeling when you fall, then to look up and see a dozen hands extended to aid you from your comrades, that is a world I wish to see in my lifetime.

It also comes to my attention that throughout the tenants, I scarcely or not at all mention women Dmitrists, this is not out of contempt for the woman, or the belief that the woman is not worthy of Dmitrism; quite the opposite is true. I merely used men as I myself am a man and it is easier to put into words. Women are indeed welcome in Dmitrism, and encouraged to take up the torch alongside men. They are capable of gaining good health, strength, industriousness, and going into space, just to name a few things I have listed in the tenants, so why shouldn't the Libertarian Man also be accompanied by the Libertarian Woman? A family unit after all is two spouses, be it two women, two men, a man and a woman. Both are equally important to society in many ways so I doubly encourage women to join the cause of liberty.

The Dmitrist should not be entirely preoccupied with work; he needs play as well to not become a 'dull boy' as the saying goes. Leisure in days off or on breaks at the factory or farms should be spent by the Dmitrist as he sees fit to increase his enjoyment of life. He should always do his very best to entertain himself, life shouldn't be all work all the time.It would become a boring existence filled with labor at all hours. The Dmitrist is proud of his labor, he loves his work, for it benefits him and his posterity. But repetition is easy to get bored with, he shouldn't shy away from modern entertainment such as films, video games, or partying. He simply needs to remember moderation in these things, as he should still aspire to become the best he can be. Some Dmitrists may find that exercise also counts as entertainment, and for those people, I applaud them.

The Action Plan Of The Dmitrist Cause

The Action plan of Dmitrism is simplistic, as it requires few steps to begin its journey towards bringing forth a united mankind and a prosperous society.

1. Begin your journey towards becoming the "libertarian man". You need to be an example of what you preach, to become the best you can be. Work hard to educate yourself, make yourself healthier, faster, stronger, well kempt. Show the world that you are the man of the future.

2. The Dmitrists must grow, they must become a force to be reckoned with. A few thousand or so Dmitrists in a single area can be enough to begin the great shift towards liberty. So that is the first step my comrades, grow our numbers. Spread propaganda, spread the tenets, debate in front of your critics, attract the onlookers to our cause. Give soapbox speeches and spark the flames of freedom in the minds of those who hear your words.

3. Begin gathering your fellow Dmitrists and buy property adjacent to one another, congregate together, and make a society from the ground up. The Dmitrists shall slowly replace the current population of the area with themselves, making it easier to cooperate and organize. Once a majority of any given region; be it a town, city, county or province, is filled with Dmitrists, invite libertarians to set up companies in the region (i.e. farms and manufacturing). Then begins step four of the plan.

4. Begin the process of self-sufficiency and militarism. The Dmitrists should start working hard to begin making capital, using the companies they invited in during step three. They should also begin making gardens for personal use if they haven't already. The Dmitrists should also start militarizing the society and setting up volunteer training facilities to teach the uneducated important lessons, such as gun safety, maintenance, target practice and weapon assembly and disassembly, and much more. Once the society is self-sufficient, exporting goods, and well defended by the people, then the rest is up to them. The Dmitrist must now stand as the vanguard of liberty and protect it. The tenants will aid them towards a new future.

Special Thanks

and honors to those who inspired me throughout my political journey and whose dreams furthered mankind's progress

A special thanks to the following people:

Ron Paul-Libertarian philosopher and politician

David Friedman- Anarchist legal philosopher

Murray Rothbard- Libertarian philosopher and founder of anarcho-capitalism

Hans hermann Hoppe- Libertarian philosopher

George Edward Griffin- Author of 'the creature from jekyll island'

Robert Heinlein- Science fiction author

Vernor Vinge-Science fiction author

James P. Hogan- Science fiction author

Eric Frank Russell- Science fiction author

Nestor Makhno- Militant Anarchist leader

Ludwig Von Mises- Libertarian economist

Larken Rose- Modern Voluntaryist philosopher and musician

Louis Lingg- Haymarket Martyr

Auberon Herbert- Founder of Voluntaryism

Harriet Tubman- Militant Abolitionist

John Brown- Militant Abolitionist

Ayn Rand- Founder of Objectivism

Samuel Edward Konkin III- Founder of Agorism

Kristopher Borer- Libertarian author

Peter Kropotkin- Anarchist, historian and philosopher

Eric July- Libertarian musician

Yuri Gagarin- First man in space

Vladimir Komarov- First man to die in space (rest in peace)

And a final thank you to Laika the dog. rest in peace little one, Your sacrifice shall not be in vain.

LIBERTY UNDER ATTACK PUBLICATIONS *tell your story*

1. **An Illusive Phantom of Hope: A Critique of Reformism** by Kyle Rearden (Audiobook/Anthology)
2. **Just Below The Surface: A Guide to Security Culture** by Kyle Rearden (Audiobook/Paperback)
3. **Sedition, Subversion, and Sabotage, Field Manual No. 1: A Three Part Solution to the State** by Ben Stone (Paperback/Audiobook)
4. **#agora** by anonymous (Paperback/Audiobook)
5. **Vonu: A Strategy for Self-Liberation** by Shane Radliff (Paperback)
6. **Second Realm: Book on Strategy** by Smuggler and XYZ (Paperback/Audiobook)
7. **Vonu: The Search for Personal Freedom** by Rayo (Special Paperback Reprint/Audiobook)
8. **Vonu: The Search for Personal Freedom, Part 2 [Letters From Rayo]** (Paperback)
9. **Going Mobile** by Tom Marshall (Paperback/Audiobook)
10. **Anarchist to Abolitionist: A Bad Quaker's Journey** by Ben Stone
11. **Brushfire, A Thriller** by Matthew Wojtecki (Paperback/Audiobook)
12. **2048 (A BRUSHFIRE THRILLER)** by Matthew Wojtecki
13. **VonuLife, March 1973** by Rayo et al (Paperback)
14. **Ocean Freedom Notes** by Jim Stumm, Rayo, et al (Paperback)
15. **The Big Book of Secret Hiding Places** by Jack Luger (Paperback)
16. **The Invention of Evil** by Henry Jones (Paperback/Kindle)

17. **Low Cost Living Notes** by Jim Stumm et al (Paperback/Kindle)
18. **Survival Gardening Notes** by Jim Stumm et al (Paperback/Kindle)
19. **The Permanent Floating Voluntary Society** by Kerry Thornley (Paperback/Kindle)
20. **A Vonu Guide to Firearms** by Josiah Warren & Shane Radliff (Paperback)

Visit <u>LibertyUnderAttack.com</u> for discounted bundles, privacy tools, and more!